Motorcycles
Inside and Out

Chris Oxlade

PowerKiDS press.

New York

Published in 2009 by The Rosen Publishing Group Inc.
29 East 21st Street, New York, NY 10010

First Edition

Senior Editor: Jennifer Schofield
Editor: Rob Scott Colson
Designer: Darren Jordan
Consultant: Ben Russell

Library of Congress Cataloging-in-Publication Data

Oxlade, Chris.
  Motorcycles inside and out / Chris Oxlade. — 1st ed.
      p. cm. — (Machines inside out)
  Includes index.
  ISBN 978-1-4358-2864-3 (library binding)
  ISBN 978-1-4358-2942-8 (paperback)
  ISBN 978-1-4358-2946-6 (6-pack)
  1. Motorcycles—Parts—Juvenile literature. 2. Motorcycles—Equipment and supplies—
  Juvenile literature. 3. Motorcycles—Juvenile literature. I. Title.
  TL440.15.09525 2009
  629.227'5--dc22
                              2008025731

Manufactured in China

Acknowledgments
Cover Shaun Lowe/istockphoto
6–7 Makoto Ouchi, 9 Makoto Ouchi, 8 Rick Friedman/Corbis, 10 Jon Patton/istockphoto, 11t Motorcycle Cruiser
Magazine, 11b Makoto Ouchi,12 Baloncici/Dreamstime.com, 13t Don Bayley/istockphoto, 13b Worlds End Motorcycles,
14–15 Dannyphoto80/Dreamstime.com, 14 MotorcycleUSA.com, 15 calculatedrisk.ca, 16–17 Makoto Ouchi,16 Judi
Ashlock/istockphoto, 17 Mark Huntington/istockphoto, 18l Kawasaki, 18r Alexey Stiop/Dreamstime.com, 19 Jarle
Eltevest, 20 Makoto Ouchi, 21b Andrew Quinlan, 21t Kerstin Klaassen/istockphoto.com, 22 Makoto Ouchi, 23b Barry
Chambers/Dreamstime.com, 23t Don Splawn, 24b Mark Atkins/Dreamstime.com, 24t Honda USA, 25 Juri
Bizgajmer/Dreamstime.com, 26 Dylan Sanchez/istockphoto.com, 27b Kawasaki, 27t Harry Starr/istockphoto

Contents

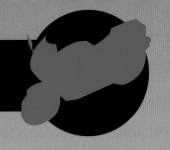

Motorcycles inside out

A motorcycle is a machine built for speed. Inside are thousands of parts, from large metal tubes in the frame, to tiny electronic components that control the engine. In this book, diagrams show you all the main parts of a motorcycle. Here you can see parts of a Yamaha sports motorcycle.

Frame and bodywork

The frame is the main part of the motorcycle. All the other parts are attached to it. The bodywork gives the motorcycle a smooth shape.

Wheels

The wheels allow the motorcycle to roll along the road. The tires grip the road and help to give the rider a smooth and safe ride.

Exhaust

The exhaust carries waste gases from the engine into the air. It also stops the blast of gases from making a roaring noise.

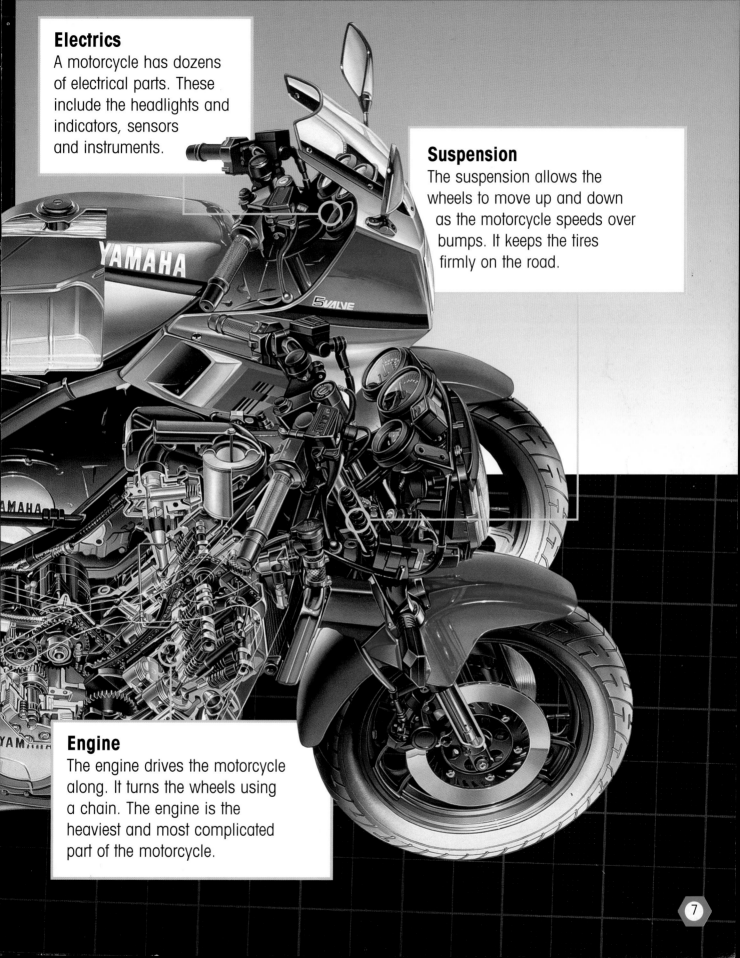

Electrics

A motorcycle has dozens of electrical parts. These include the headlights and indicators, sensors and instruments.

Suspension

The suspension allows the wheels to move up and down as the motorcycle speeds over bumps. It keeps the tires firmly on the road.

Engine

The engine drives the motorcycle along. It turns the wheels using a chain. The engine is the heaviest and most complicated part of the motorcycle.

Motorcycle frame

A motorcycle has a strong frame that stretches from the handlebars back to the rider's seat and down to the engine. The frame is made from steel, aluminum, or an alloy. It is made up of pieces welded together at their ends. The frame is sometimes called the chassis (say SHA-SEE).

Adding parts

The frame is like the skeleton of a motorcycle. It supports all the other parts and holds them in place. Parts are bolted onto it at various attachment points. Here, parts are being added to a frame on the production line at the Harley Davidson factory in Wisconsin.

TECH FACT

It is important that the frame does not bend, even a tiny bit. A stiff frame keeps the wheels in line with each other. This gives the motorcycle good handling, which means it feels easy to ride. A motorcycle with poor handling is hard to steer around corners, and can feel wobbly.

Frame spars

The most common frame for sports motorcycles has two pieces of metal called spars, one on each side of the motorcycle. They stretch from the steering head, around the engine, and finish at the swing-arm attachment that supports the back wheel.

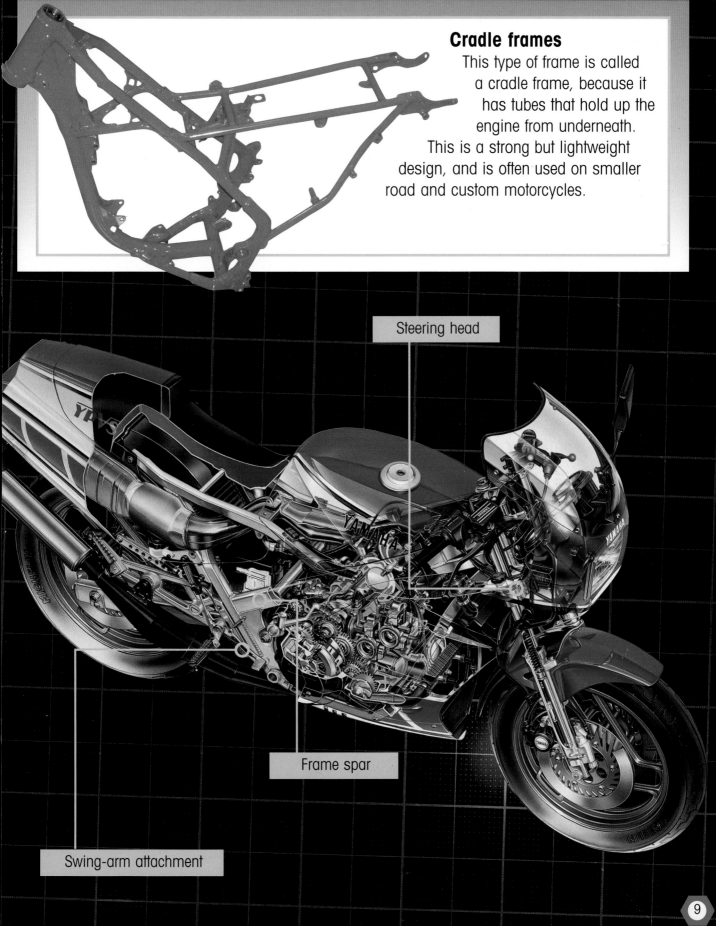

Cradle frames

This type of frame is called a cradle frame, because it has tubes that hold up the engine from underneath. This is a strong but lightweight design, and is often used on smaller road and custom motorcycles.

Steering head

Frame spar

Swing-arm attachment

Wheels and suspension

A motorcycle's wheels allow it to roll smoothly along the road. The vehicle is supported over the wheels by the suspension. The suspension allows the wheels to move up and down as they go over bumps. This keeps the tires on the road and also gives the rider a comfortable ride.

Suspension units

Suspension units are made up of a spring and a shock absorber. There are two units for the front wheel in the front forks. There are either one or two units attached to the rear wheel, depending on the model of motorcycle.

Front fork

Forks and arms

The front forks link the handlebars and the front wheel. Each fork contains a telescopic suspension unit. The rear wheel is on a swing arm. A suspension unit controls how far it swings up and down.

Tires

The job of the tires is to grip the road. They let the bike accelerate, brake, and corner safely. The tires are made from rubber, strengthened with thin layers of steel. The tread pushes any water on the road out from under the tire.

TECH FACT

A suspension unit's spring supports the weight of the motorcycle above it. When the rider gets on, the springs squash a little more with the extra weight. The shock absorber stops the spring from squashing or stretching too much. It also stops the motorcycle from bouncing up and down after a bump.

Front fork

Swing arm

Engine parts

The engine turns the rear wheel, which makes the motorcycle move along. Big bikes have engines with the same power as the engines in a small car. Cylinders are spaces inside the engine, about the shape and size of tin cans. Pistons fit snugly inside the cylinders, and slide up and down them.

Cylinders and pistons

Fuel burns inside the cylinders, pushing the pistons down their cylinders. Each piston has a connecting rod that pushes a crankshaft around. The crankshaft is connected to the wheels. Valves, operated by the camshaft, open to let fuel into the cylinders.

TECH FACT

The power of an engine depends on its capacity and how fast it turns. The capacity is the total space inside the cylinders. It ranges from 50 cc (cubic centimeters) in single-cylinder engines, to more than 1000 cc in multiple-cylinder engines. The faster an engine can turn, the more power it sends to the wheels.

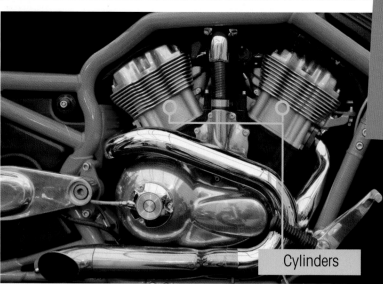

Cylinders

Engine layouts

The engine in the main picture, right, has four cylinders, two on each side, arranged in a V-shape. It is known as a V-4 engine. The engine above is a V-twin, with two cylinders. This is a classic engine layout used on many American motorcycles.

Opposed engines

The photograph, right, shows one cylinder of an opposed twin engine. The two cylinders are opposite each other, one on each side of the motorcycle. There are also opposed fours, sixes, and even eights. Opposed engines are also called boxer engines.

Cylinder

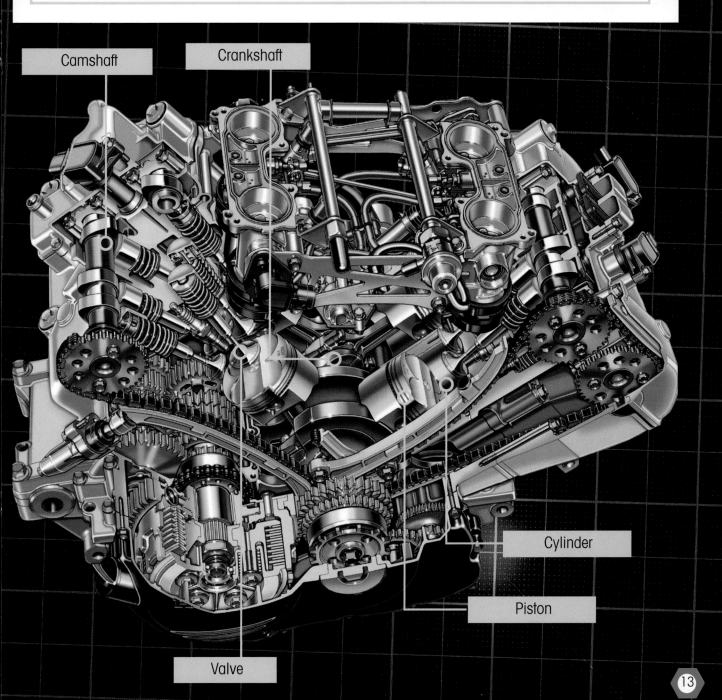

Camshaft

Crankshaft

Cylinder

Piston

Valve

How an engine works

As a motorcycle engine runs, each cylinder follows a sequence of moves. In most motorcycle engines, the sequence is the four-stroke cycle. Each piston goes in and out of its cylinder twice during the sequence. Valves open to let a mixture of fuel and air into the cylinders. Other valves open to let exhaust gases out. The fuel is ignited (set on fire) electrically by a spark plug.

Valve

Spark plug

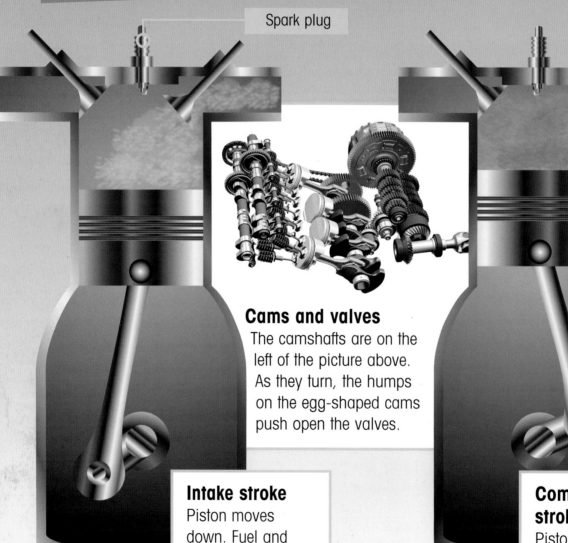

Cams and valves
The camshafts are on the left of the picture above. As they turn, the humps on the egg-shaped cams push open the valves.

Intake stroke
Piston moves down. Fuel and air mixture is sucked into the cylinder.

Compression stroke
Piston moves up. Fuel and air are squeezed into the top of the cylinder.

Perfect timing

This cutaway engine shows the camshafts, valves, and cylinder. The camshafts are turned by a belt from the engine, and make the valves open and close at the right time during the cycle. The spark plugs work electrically. The plug produces a tiny spark that ignites the fuel.

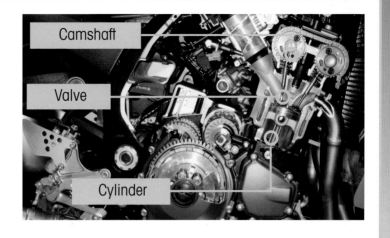

Camshaft

Valve

Cylinder

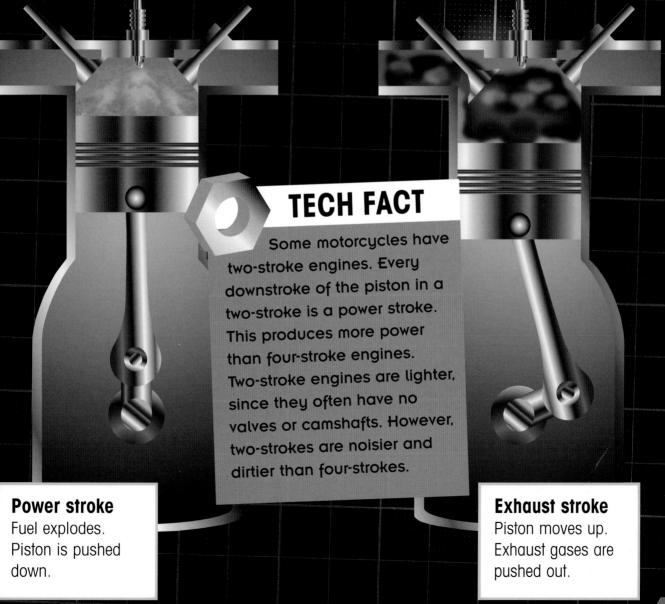

TECH FACT

Some motorcycles have two-stroke engines. Every downstroke of the piston in a two-stroke is a power stroke. This produces more power than four-stroke engines. Two-stroke engines are lighter, since they often have no valves or camshafts. However, two-strokes are noisier and dirtier than four-strokes.

Power stroke
Fuel explodes. Piston is pushed down.

Exhaust stroke
Piston moves up. Exhaust gases are pushed out.

Fuel and exhaust

A motorcycle engine needs fuel to work. The fuel is mixed with air and burns inside the cylinders. The fuel is stored in the fuel tank and pumped along pipes to the engine. The burning fuel makes waste gases that are carried away by the exhaust system.

Exhaust parts

The exhaust system carries exhaust gases to the rear of the motorcycle, where they go into the air. The silencer muffles blasts of exhaust gas in the exhaust pipes. This stops the motorcycle making a loud noise.

The throttle

A motorcycle rider twists the throttle on the right-hand handlebar to make the engine give out more power. The throttle allows more air and fuel to reach the cylinders. This makes the burning fuel push the pistons harder. So the engine speeds up, making the motorcycle go faster.

TECH FACT

Some big sports and touring motorcycles have sophisticated engine management electronics. The electronics make the engine work very efficiently. They control the amount of fuel that goes into the cylinders, when the spark plug makes its spark, and when the valves open and close.

Right-hand handlebar

Throttle

Carburetor

A motorcycle's carburetor is where fuel is mixed with air. The mixture then goes into the cylinders. Many modern motorcycles do not have a carburetor. Instead, the fuel is injected straight into the cylinders.

Fuel tank

Exhaust pipe

Silencer

Cooling the engine

When a motorcycle engine is running, it makes dozens of strokes every second, and the engine parts rub against each other at great speed. The burning fuel and rubbing generate a lot of heat. Too much heat would make the engine stop working, so the heat must be removed. This is the job of the cooling system.

Liquid cooling
Most large modern motorcycle engines are cooled by water. The water flows through pipes inside the engine, carrying the heat away. The water is cooled in the radiator before it flows back to the engine.

Air cooling
Some motorcycle engines are cooled by air. The cylinders have wide fins on their outsides, which get hot. As the motorcycle speeds up, air cools the fins down.

Radiator
Hot water from the engine flows into hundreds of thin pipes in the radiator. Air flowing between the pipes cools the water.

TECH FACT
Engines are filled with engine oil. The oil reduces friction by letting the engine parts move smoothly against each other. If the oil or cooling water leaks away, the engine quickly gets very hot. The parts expand and jam against each other, and the engine seizes up.

Radiator

Cooling water pipe

Water pump

Transmission

A motorcycle's transmission connects the engine to the rear wheel. It is made up of the clutch, the gearbox, and the chain. The transmission allows the rider to start and stop the motorcycle, and ride at different speeds without the engine running too slowly or quickly.

Chain

Rear sprocket

Gearbox

Chain drive

There are toothed wheels called sprockets on the gearbox and the rear wheel. They are linked by a chain, so that the gearbox can turn the wheel. A few touring motorcycles have a shaft drive instead of chain drive.

Sprocket

Chain

Gears and clutch

Gears change how fast the engine turns the rear wheel. Low gears are used for starting off or riding slowly, high gears for fast riding. The clutch disconnects the gearbox from the engine before changing gear.

TECH FACT

Motorcycles have sequential gears. The rider lifts the gear-change pedal to change up a gear, and presses down to change down a gear. The rider must change gear in order, or sequence. This is different from a manual car, where the driver can change from any gear to any other gear by using the stick shift.

The gearbox

The gearbox contains cogs on two shafts. One shaft is turned by the engine and the other turns the rear wheel (via the chain). When the rider selects a gear, a cog on one shaft interlocks with a cog on the other shaft.

Main shaft turned by engine

Shaft to rear wheel

Steering and brakes

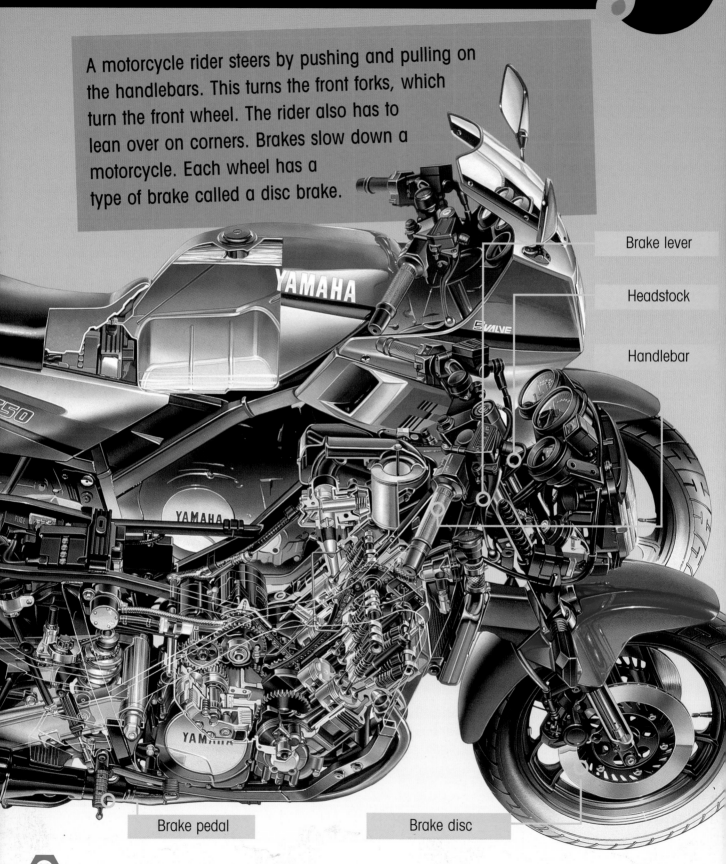

A motorcycle rider steers by pushing and pulling on the handlebars. This turns the front forks, which turn the front wheel. The rider also has to lean over on corners. Brakes slow down a motorcycle. Each wheel has a type of brake called a disc brake.

Brake lever

Headstock

Handlebar

Brake pedal

Brake disc

YAMAHA

5 VALVE

The headstock

The front forks are joined to the motorcycle frame at the headstock. The headstock stops the forks from wobbling, but lets them twist from side to side. This is very important for controlling the bike, especially at high speeds.

Headstock

Discs and pads

There is a metal disc attached to each wheel. A calliper unit is attached to the front forks and to the rear swing arm. This contains two brake pads. When the rider applies the brakes, the pads squeeze the disc, which slows the wheel.

Brake controls

The front brake is applied by a lever on the right-hand handlebar, and the rear brake is applied by the right foot pedal. On small motorcycles, the brakes are operated by cables. Larger types use fluid in pipes.

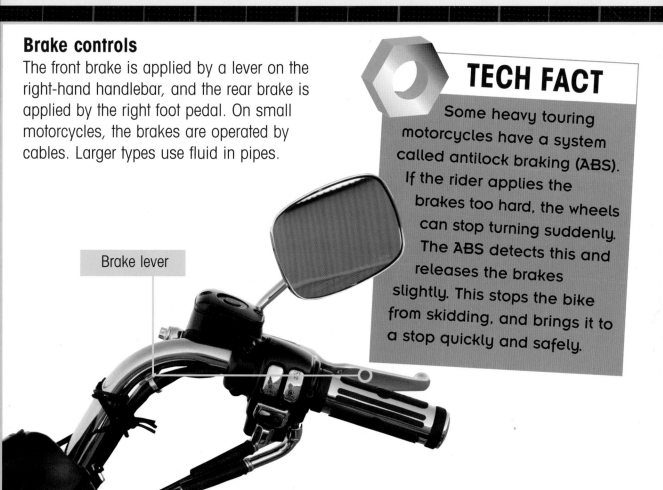

Brake lever

TECH FACT

Some heavy touring motorcycles have a system called antilock braking (ABS). If the rider applies the brakes too hard, the wheels can stop turning suddenly. The ABS detects this and releases the brakes slightly. This stops the bike from skidding, and brings it to a stop quickly and safely.

Safety and comfort

Motorcycles have several features to make their riders as safe as possible. For example, some large models have antilock brakes (see page 23), and motorcycles can be fitted with sidebars to protect the rider's legs if the motorcycle topples over. Riders' clothing and other equipment also help to keep them safe and comfortable.

Protective clothes

Motorcycling clothing is designed to protect riders from the wind and rain, and from bumps and scrapes if they fall off their bikes. Jackets and pants are made from leather or artificial fabrics. There is extra padding at the knees, elbows, and shoulders. The helmet protects the head and is the most important piece of safety equipment.

Air bags

The Honda Gold Wing is the only motorcycle to have an air bag for the rider. There are sensors in the front forks that can tell if the front wheel hits something at high speed. The air bag then automatically inflates to stop the rider flying over the handlebars.

Taking passengers

Many motorycles have a seat large enough for two people. The passenger is said to be riding pillion. He or she holds onto a bar behind the seat, and must keep very still around corners so that the motorcycle handles smoothly.

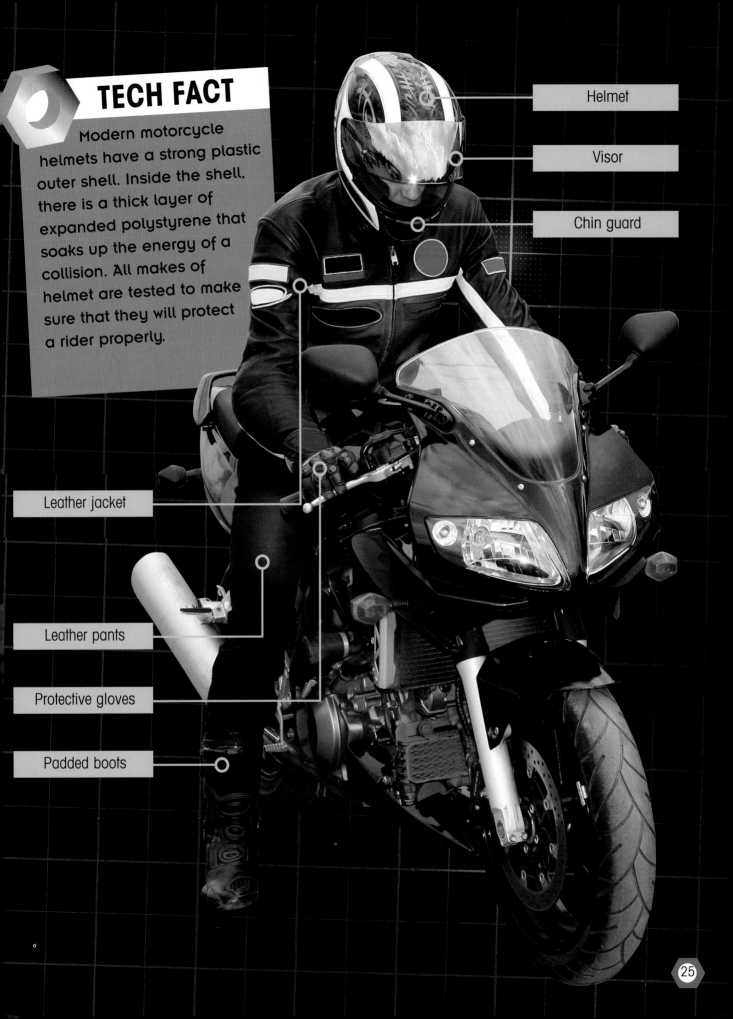

TECH FACT

Modern motorcycle helmets have a strong plastic outer shell. Inside the shell, there is a thick layer of expanded polystyrene that soaks up the energy of a collision. All makes of helmet are tested to make sure that they will protect a rider properly.

Helmet

Visor

Chin guard

Leather jacket

Leather pants

Protective gloves

Padded boots

Quads

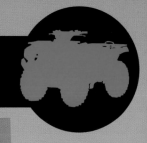

A quad is an off-road vehicle. It is a cross between a motorcycle and a small car. The word quad means "four," and quads have four wheels. Most quads are made by regular motorcycle manufacturers, such as Honda, Yamaha, and Kawasaki. The proper name for a quad is an all-terrain vehicle (ATV for short).

Motorcycle features

Quads have motorcycle engines. The rider sits astride the vehicle, with one leg on each side. The controls are similar to the controls on a motorcycle. The rider steers with handlebars, which turn the front wheels.

TECH FACT

Quads have engines very similar to motorcycle engines. They are either four-stroke or two-stroke, and range in capacity from 50 cc to 1000 cc. Sports quads have large two-stroke engines for maximum power. Most utility quads have four-wheel drive, and most sports quads have two-wheel drive.

Quad suspension

Each wheel on a quad has its own suspension unit, with a spring and shock absorber. Here the suspension units are painted yellow.

Sports and utility

The two main types of quads are sports and utility. Sports quads are designed for racing on dirt, mud, and sand. Utility quads are designed for farm transportation and construction sites. Sports quads are light and powerful, and can travel up to 93 mph (150 km/h).

Engine cover

Rider's seat

Engine protector

Equipment rack

Low-pressure tires

Mud guard

Glossary

Accelerate
To speed up.

Alloy
A material made from two metals or a metal mixed with another material.

Cog
A wheel with teeth around its edge.

Component
An object that is part of a larger, more complex machine.

Cylinder
A space inside an engine where fuel burns.

Exhaust
The parts of a motorcycle that carry waste gases away from the engine.

Four-stroke
An engine in which there is a power stroke on every other downstroke of the pistons.

Frame
The main part of a motorcycle, which keeps the vehicle rigid and supports all the other parts.

Hydraulic
Describes a machine that has parts moved by liquid pumped along pipes.

Piston
Part of an engine that slides up and down a cylinder.

Sensor
A device that detects things, such as the temperature in an engine or when a fuel tank is empty.

Shock absorber
Part of the suspension that stops the spring from getting too squashed or stretched.

Skid
When a motorcycle slides along the road without one or both of the wheels turning. A skid happens when the tires lose their grip on the road.

Suspension
Part of a motorcycle that lets the wheels move up and down as the motorcycle goes over bumps.

Suspension unit
Part of a motorcycle's suspension, made up of a spring and a shock absorber.

Swing arm
The part of a motorcycle suspension that connects the rear wheel to the frame. The swing arm lets the rear wheel move up and down.

Two-stroke
An engine in which there is a power stroke on every downstroke of the pistons.

Valve
Part of an engine that opens temporarily to let fuel into a cylinder or exhaust gases out of a cylinder.

Welding
A way of joining two pieces of metal together by heating them up until they melt, and pressing them together so that they form a strong joint.

Further reading

The Need for Speed: Motorbikes
by Philip Raby and Simon Nix
(LernerSports, 1999)

On the Tracks: Motorcycle Mania
by David Armentrout
(Rourke Publishing, 2007)

World's Greatest Motorbikes
by Ian Graham
(Raintree, 2005)

Web Sites

Due to the changing nature of Internet links, PowerKids Press has developed an online list of Web sites related to the subject of this book. This site is updated regularly. Please use this link to access this list:
www.powerkidslinks.com/mio/motorcy

Index